HOW TO CARE

MW01229102

INTRODUCTION

Congratulations! You're the proud caregiver of an octogenarian - a person who has lived through eight decades of history, witnessed countless changes, and accumulated more wisdom than you can shake a stick at. But let's face it: caring for an elderly loved one is no easy feat. From navigating health issues and cognitive decline to adapting your home and providing emotional support, caregiving can be a challenging and rewarding experience all at once.

That's why we wrote this book - to help you navigate the ups and downs of caring for your octogenarian with humor, compassion, and a healthy dose of wit. Whether you're a seasoned caregiver or just starting out, this book is for you.

So, what exactly is an octogenarian? Put simply, it's someone who has lived for 80 years or more. But as you'll soon discover, being an octogenarian is about more than just age - it's a mindset. Octogenarians have seen it all, done it all, and have a unique perspective on life that only comes with experience. They may be slowing down physically, but mentally, they're as sharp as ever. And that's where you come in - to help them live their best life in their golden years.

In this book, we'll cover everything you need to know about caring for your octogenarian, from understanding their mindset and navigating physical and cognitive changes to creating a safe and comfortable living environment and keeping your loved one active and engaged. But we'll also sprinkle in some humor and anecdotes along the way, because let's be real - laughter is the best medicine, especially when it comes to caregiving.

So, buckle up and get ready for a wild ride. Caring for an octogenarian may not always be easy, but with the right mindset and a healthy sense of humor, it can be one of the most rewarding experiences of your life. Let's get started!

Why Octogenarians Need Special Care

Let's face it - octogenarians are a unique breed. They've lived through more history than you can shake a stick at, and they've got the stories to prove it. But with age comes a whole host of challenges - physical, cognitive, and emotional - that require special care and attention.

First off, let's talk about the physical stuff. As we age, our bodies start to slow down, creak, and ache in all sorts of weird and wonderful ways. For octogenarians, this can mean everything from arthritis and joint pain to vision and hearing loss. They may move a little slower and need extra assistance with tasks that were once second nature. But fear not! With a little creativity and some assistive devices (think walkers, canes, and hearing aids), your octogenarian can still lead a fulfilling and independent life.

Of course, physical challenges are just the tip of the iceberg. Cognitive decline is another biggie when it comes to caring for octogenarians. Memory loss, dementia, and Alzheimer's are all common issues that require special care and attention. But here's the thing - just because someone has a cognitive impairment doesn't mean they've lost their sense of humor or their love for life. In fact, sometimes it's the opposite - a good laugh can work wonders in lifting spirits and promoting mental well-being.

Last but not least, let's talk about the emotional side of things. As we age, our social networks may start to shrink, leaving us feeling isolated and lonely. This is especially true for octogenarians who may have lost friends and loved ones along the way. That's why it's so important to provide emotional support and companionship for your octogenarian.

Whether it's sharing a cup of tea and a good book or going on a wild adventure, spending quality time with your loved one can make all the difference in the world.

So, there you have it - a brief overview of why octogenarians need special care. It's not always easy, but with a little patience, creativity, and a good sense of humor, you can provide the love and support your octogenarian needs to thrive in their golden years. Now, let's get to it!

B. The Importance of Humor and Compassion in Caregiving

The Importance of Humor and Compassion in Caregiving or, Why Laughter is the Best Medicine.

Let's face it - caregiving is hard work. It can be physically and emotionally draining, and it's easy to get bogged down in the day-to-day challenges of caring for an octogenarian. But here's the thing - humor and compassion can be powerful tools in making caregiving a little easier and a lot more enjoyable.

First off, let's talk about humor. When you're caring for an octogenarian, there are bound to be some hilarious moments along the way. Whether it's a witty quip from your loved one or a silly mishap that has you both in stitches, laughter can be a great way to break up the monotony of daily caregiving tasks.

Plus, it's a great stress-reliever - studies have shown that laughter can boost endorphins and reduce stress hormones, making it a natural mood-booster.

But humor isn't just about making light of tough situations. It can also be a way to connect with your loved one and show them that you're there for them, no matter what. Sharing a joke or a funny story can be a great way to bond and create positive memories together.

Next up, let's talk about compassion. When you're caring for an octogenarian, it's important to remember that they're more than just a set of physical and cognitive challenges.

They're a whole person, with a lifetime of experiences, emotions, and dreams. Compassion means seeing your loved one as a whole person and treating them with the respect and dignity they deserve.

Compassion can take many forms, from simple acts of kindness (like bringing your loved one their favorite snack or helping them with a crossword puzzle) to more complex emotional support (like listening to their fears and concerns and offering reassurance). Whatever form it takes, compassion is a key ingredient in successful caregiving.

So, the importance of humor and compassion in caregiving. Whether you're cracking jokes or offering a shoulder to cry on, these two qualities can make all the difference in providing the best possible care for your octogenarian.

So go ahead, laugh a little, show a lot of love, and let's make caregiving a little less daunting and a lot more fun!

UNDERSTANDING THE OCTOGENARIAN MINDSET

When it comes to octogenarians, the old adage "age is just a number" couldn't be more true. These wise and wonderful individuals have lived through more than most of us can imagine, and their perspective on life is something to be cherished. But if you want to provide the best possible care for your octogenarian, you need to understand their unique mindset.

First off, let's talk about memory. As we age, our memory can start to slip a little. For octogenarians, this can mean forgetting where they put their glasses, or even what day it is. But here's the thing - just because they may forget things doesn't mean they're not still sharp as a tack. In fact, some of the most insightful and witty comments can come from octogenarians who have seen it all and aren't afraid to speak their minds.

Next up, let's talk about routines. Octogenarians can be creatures of habit, and they may have a particular routine or schedule that they like to stick to. Whether it's breakfast at 7am sharp or a daily afternoon nap, these routines can provide a sense of comfort and security for your loved one. So if you're planning on changing things up, be sure to do so gradually and with plenty of communication.

Of course, routines aren't the only thing to keep in mind when it comes to the octogenarian mindset. Emotions can also play a big role in how your loved one perceives the world around them. They may feel more vulnerable or anxious than they did when they were younger, or they may be dealing with grief or loss that can affect their mood. Being aware of these emotions and providing emotional support can be key in helping your loved one feel safe and cared for.

Last but not least, let's talk about humor. As we mentioned earlier, humor can be a powerful tool in connecting with your loved one and making caregiving a little easier. But it's important to remember that everyone has a different sense of humor, and what may be funny to you may not be funny to your octogenarian. So be mindful of their preferences and tailor your humor accordingly.

Understanding where your loved one is coming from can help you provide the best possible care and create positive memories together. So go forth, be patient, be kind, and let's learn from these amazing individuals who have so much wisdom to offer.

Common Attitudes and Beliefs Among Octogenarians

Octogenarians are a special breed. They've seen it all and they know what they like. If you're lucky enough to care for an octogenarian, you'll quickly learn that there are certain attitudes and beliefs that are common among this age group.

First up, let's talk about frugality. Octogenarians are notorious for being thrifty, and they've got some tricks up their sleeves when it comes to saving a buck. Whether it's reusing tea bags or saving aluminum foil, they know how to stretch a dollar. And who knows, maybe they're onto something - after all, being frugal can be good for the planet and your wallet!

Next, let's talk about technology. Now, we all know that technology is constantly changing and evolving. But for octogenarians, it can be a whole other world. They may be resistant to new gadgets or find them overwhelming.

But here's the thing - technology can be a great way to stay connected with loved ones and the world around us. So if your octogenarian is hesitant to try something new, maybe offer to show them the ropes and see if they warm up to it.

Of course, attitudes and beliefs can also be influenced by past experiences. Octogenarians may have lived through wars, social movements, and economic changes that have shaped their worldview. They may have strong opinions on politics, social issues, or cultural norms.

While you may not always agree with their views, it's important to respect them and listen to their perspective. After all, they've got a lifetime of experience to draw from.

Last but not least, let's talk about independence. Octogenarians may be slowing down physically, but that doesn't mean they've lost their sense of independence. They may resist help or feel frustrated by limitations.

But with a little creativity and patience, you can find ways to support their independence while also ensuring their safety and wellbeing.

Here are a few more tips for understanding common attitudes and beliefs among octogenarians:

Respect their routines: Octogenarians often value routine and predictability in their daily lives. They may have specific times for meals, medication, and other activities. Try to accommodate their routines as much as possible to provide a sense of stability and comfort.

Be patient with memory loss: Memory loss is a common issue among the elderly, and it can be frustrating for both the octogenarian and the caregiver.

Try to be patient and understanding when they forget things or repeat themselves. Reminiscing about the past can be a great way to connect with them and trigger memories.

Keep them engaged: Octogenarians may feel isolated or lonely, especially if they have mobility or health issues. Keeping them engaged in social activities, hobbies, or interests can help prevent depression and improve their quality of life.

Emphasize safety: While independence is important, safety should always be a top priority. Make sure the octogenarian's living space is safe and accessible, and consider assistive devices or modifications if necessary. Encourage them to ask for help when needed, and be available to provide assistance as needed.

Stay positive: A positive attitude can go a long way in caregiving. Even when things are challenging, try to stay optimistic and find humor in everyday situations. Laughter can be a great way to relieve stress and connect with your loved one.

Remember, caring for an octogenarian can be both challenging and rewarding. By understanding their mindset and beliefs, you can provide compassionate care and build a strong relationship based on trust and respect.

How to Communicate Effectively with Octogenarians

Communicating with octogenarians can sometimes feel like speaking a different language. But with a little patience and understanding, you can learn to bridge the generation gap and communicate effectively. Here are some tips to get you started:

Speak clearly and slowly: Many octogenarians have hearing loss, so it's important to speak clearly and at a slower pace. Avoid shouting or speaking too loudly, as this can be uncomfortable or even painful for them.

Use simple language: Complex or technical language can be confusing or overwhelming for octogenarians. Try to use simple, everyday language that they can easily understand.

Ask open-ended questions: Instead of asking yes-or-no questions, try to ask open-ended questions that encourage conversation. For example, instead of asking "Do you feel okay?", ask "How are you feeling today?"

Listen actively: Listening is an essential part of effective communication. Take the time to listen actively to what the octogenarian is saying, and show that you're interested and engaged in the conversation.

Use humor: Humor can be a great way to connect with octogenarians and lighten the mood. Jokes, funny stories, or reminiscing about the past can all be great ways to inject some humor into the conversation.

Be patient: Remember, communication with octogenarians can take a little extra time and effort. Be patient and don't rush the conversation. Take the time to let them express themselves fully and respond thoughtfully.

By following these tips, you can learn to speak "elderly" and communicate effectively with your loved one. And who knows, you might even learn a thing or two from their lifetime of experience and wisdom!

Here are a few more tips for communicating effectively with octogenarians:

Use visual aids: Visual aids, such as pictures, diagrams, or written instructions, can be helpful for explaining complex concepts or procedures.

They can also be useful for overcoming language barriers, as many older adults may struggle with reading or understanding written instructions.

Avoid talking down to them: While it's important to use simple language, it's equally important to treat octogenarians with respect and dignity. Avoid speaking to them as if they were children, and instead treat them as the intelligent, capable adults they are.

Find common ground: Try to find common interests or experiences that you can both relate to. For example, if your loved one served in the military, you might ask them about their experiences or share stories of your own relatives who served.

Be aware of cultural differences: Older adults may come from different cultural backgrounds, and it's important to be respectful and aware of these differences. Learn about their cultural traditions and customs, and try to incorporate them into your interactions when appropriate.

Avoid interrupting: Interrupting can be rude or frustrating for anyone, but it can be especially difficult for older adults who may take longer to express themselves. Be patient and wait for them to finish speaking before responding.

Remember, effective communication is key to building a strong and positive relationship with your loved one. By taking the time to listen, understand, and connect with them, you can provide compassionate care and improve their overall well-being.

NAVIGATING PHYSICAL AND COGNITIVE CHANGES

As we age, our bodies and minds undergo a variety of changes, and octogenarians are no exception. From wrinkles to forgetfulness, there are many physical and cognitive changes that octogenarians may experience. Here are some tips for navigating these changes with humor and grace:

Embrace the wrinkles: Let's face it, wrinkles are a fact of life. But instead of trying to hide them or feel self-conscious about them, try to embrace them as a sign of a life well-lived. After all, each wrinkle tells a story!

Stay active: Regular exercise can help keep both the body and mind healthy and strong. Encourage your loved one to stay active with activities that they enjoy, such as walking, yoga, or dancing.

Be patient with forgetfulness: Memory loss and forgetfulness can be frustrating for both octogenarians and their caregivers. But instead of getting frustrated, try to be patient and understanding. Use reminders or cues to help jog their memory, and try to keep a sense of humor about it all.

Keep things simple: As cognitive function declines, it may become more difficult for octogenarians to process complex information or instructions. Keep things simple and straightforward, and break down tasks into smaller, more manageable steps.

Laugh often: Laughter truly is the best medicine, and it can be especially helpful for older adults who may be facing physical or cognitive challenges. Try to find the humor in everyday situations, and share a laugh with your loved one as often as possible.

Navigating physical and cognitive changes can be a challenge, but with a little humor and patience, you can help your loved one maintain their independence and quality of life. And who knows, you might even learn a thing or two from their years of experience and wisdom!

Common health issues among Octogenarians and How to Address Them

As we age, our bodies become more prone to certain health issues, and octogenarians are no exception. From arthritis to heart disease, there are a variety of health concerns that may arise as we enter our golden years. Here are some tips for addressing these issues with humor and insight:

Arthritis: Arthritis is a common condition that can cause pain, stiffness, and swelling in the joints. To help manage arthritis, encourage your loved one to stay active with gentle exercises such as swimming or yoga. Heat therapy, such as warm compresses or a heating pad, can also be helpful in reducing pain and stiffness.

Vision and hearing loss: As we age, our vision and hearing may decline. To help address these issues, encourage your loved one to get regular eye and hearing exams, and to wear glasses or hearing aids as needed. Make sure their living space is well-lit and free of obstacles that could cause falls.

Heart disease: Heart disease is a leading cause of death among older adults. To help prevent heart disease, encourage your loved one to maintain a healthy diet, exercise regularly, and manage their blood pressure and cholesterol levels. Make sure they have access to regular medical check-ups and screenings.

Cognitive decline: Cognitive decline, including memory loss and dementia, is a common concern among older adults. To help address these issues, encourage your loved one to stay mentally active with puzzles, games, or other stimulating activities.

Make sure they have a structured routine and access to regular social interaction.

Depression: Depression is a common concern among older adults, particularly those who may be dealing with chronic health issues or social isolation. To help address depression, encourage your loved one to stay engaged with hobbies, friends, and family. Talk to them about their feelings and make sure they have access to mental health support if needed.

Osteoporosis: Osteoporosis is a condition that causes the bones to become weaker and more prone to fractures. To help prevent osteoporosis, encourage your loved one to get enough calcium and vitamin D through diet or supplements. Weight-bearing exercises, such as walking or strength training, can also help build bone density.

Chronic pain: Chronic pain is a common concern among older adults, particularly those with conditions such as arthritis or fibromyalgia. To help manage chronic pain, encourage your loved one to try non-medical approaches such as physical therapy, acupuncture, or mindfulness practices. Make sure they have access to pain medications if needed, but be aware of the potential risks and side effects.

Incontinence: Incontinence, or loss of bladder or bowel control, can be a challenging and embarrassing issue for older adults. To help manage incontinence, encourage your loved one to practice pelvic floor exercises or to use incontinence products such as pads or briefs. Make sure their living space is easily accessible and that they have easy access to bathrooms.

Falls: Falls are a common concern among older adults, and can cause serious injuries such as broken bones or head trauma. To help prevent falls, make sure your loved one's living space is free of clutter and hazards, such as loose rugs or uneven flooring.

Encourage them to use assistive devices such as canes or walkers if needed, and make sure they have access to physical therapy to improve balance and strength.

Sleep disturbances: Sleep disturbances, including insomnia or sleep apnea, can be a common issue among older adults. To help address sleep disturbances, encourage your loved one to establish a regular sleep routine, and to create a calm and comfortable sleeping environment.

Talk to their healthcare provider about potential treatments such as medication or CPAP therapy.

Addressing common health issues among octogenarians may require some creativity and patience, but with the right approach, you can help keep your loved one healthy and thriving.

And who knows, they might even teach you a thing or two about resilience and the power of a positive attitude!

Coping with Memory Loss and Cognitive Decline

Ah, memory loss and cognitive decline - the classic struggles of aging. But fear not! As a caregiver, I'm here to help you navigate these challenges with humor and grace.

First things first, let's acknowledge that memory loss and cognitive decline can be scary and frustrating for both the octogenarian and their caregiver. It's important to approach these issues with compassion and understanding.

One helpful tip is to create a routine and stick to it. This can help reduce confusion and increase feelings of security for your loved one. Plus, who doesn't love a good routine? It's like having your own personal schedule superstar.

Another strategy is to break down tasks into smaller steps. For example, if your loved one is struggling to follow a recipe, try breaking it down into individual steps or using visual aids to help them understand the process. Plus, cooking together can be a fun and rewarding activity - just be prepared for a few burnt cookies along the way.

It's also important to encourage your loved one to stay mentally active. Activities such as puzzles, reading, or playing games can help keep the brain sharp and engaged. And who knows, you might even learn a few new board games yourself!

Finally, don't forget to take care of yourself as well. Caregiving can be a tough job, and it's important to take breaks and prioritize self-care.

Whether it's taking a yoga class or enjoying a bubble bath, make sure you're taking care of your own mental health so that you can be the best caregiver possible.

Remember, coping with memory loss and cognitive decline can be challenging, but with a little humor, compassion, and creativity, you and your octogenarian loved one can tackle these issues together.

CREATING A SAFE AND COMFORTABLE LIVING ENVIRONMENT

Well, well, well, looks like you've got an octogenarian on your hands! Congrats, you've got a wise and experienced human being in your midst. But let's face it, as we age, our needs change, and that means it's time to make some changes around the house to keep your octogenarian safe and comfortable.

First things first, let's talk about tripping hazards. You don't want your wise elder stumbling over a rug or slipping on a banana peel (I know, who still leaves banana peels lying around, right?). So, let's get rid of those hazards and make sure that the floors are slip-resistant. You know what they say, a safe floor is a happy floor.

Next up, let's talk about seating. No one wants to sit in a hard, uncomfortable chair, especially when they're in their golden years. So, let's invest in a nice, plush recliner where your octogenarian can kick back, relax, and watch some daytime TV. And while we're at it, let's make sure that the bed is comfortable too. You want your wise elder to wake up feeling rested and refreshed, not like they've been sleeping on a pile of rocks.

Now, let's talk about lighting. You don't want your octogenarian to be stumbling around in the dark trying to find the light switch, do you? Of course not! Let's install some motion-sensor lights so that they can always see where they're going. And if you really want to go all out, you can even get some smart bulbs that can be controlled with a voice command.

And finally, let's talk about technology. Just because your octogenarian is in their golden years doesn't mean they can't keep up with the latest gadgets. In fact, there are all sorts of tech out there that can help keep them safe and comfortable.

You can invest in a personal emergency response system so that they can call for help if they need it. Or you can get them a smart thermostat so that they can control the temperature without having to get up.

So there you have it, folks! Creating a safe and comfortable living environment for your octogenarian isn't rocket science, it just takes a little bit of effort and some thoughtful consideration. By following these simple steps, you'll be able to keep your wise elder safe and comfortable for years to come.

Adapting Your Home to the Needs of an Octogenarian

Well, well, well, looks like you've got an octogenarian moving in! Congrats, you're about to add some serious wisdom and life experience to your household. But let's be real, as we age, our needs change, and that means it's time to adapt your home to keep your octogenarian safe and comfortable.

First things first, let's talk about stairs. You know what they say, stairs are the ultimate nemesis of octogenarians. So, let's make sure those stairs are safe and easy to navigate.

That means installing railings, adding non-slip treads, and maybe even investing in a stairlift. Hey, if it's good enough for Grandma, it's good enough for us.

Next up, let's talk about the bathroom. You don't want your wise elder slipping and sliding around in the shower like a drunken sailor, do you? Of course not! So, let's install some grab bars, a non-slip mat, and maybe even a shower seat. Trust us, your octogenarian will thank you for it.

Now, let's talk about lighting. You don't want your octogenarian fumbling around in the dark trying to find the light switch, do you? Of course not! So, let's make sure there's plenty of lighting throughout the house, especially in high-traffic areas like the hallways and stairs. And if you really want to go all out, you can even invest in some smart bulbs that can be controlled with a voice command.

And finally, let's talk about technology. You may think your octogenarian is a tech dinosaur, but they're probably more savvy than you think. There are all sorts of tech out there that can help keep them safe and comfortable. You can invest in a personal emergency response system so that they can call for help if they need it. Or you can get them a smart speaker so that they can control the lights, thermostat, and even the TV with just their voice.

So there you have it, folks! Adapting your home to the needs of your octogenarian is a little bit of work, but it's well worth it to keep your wise elder safe and comfortable. By following these simple steps, you'll be able to create a home that's perfect for your octogenarian.

Making Your Home a Fun and Entertaining place for Your Octogenarian Loved One

Ah, the octogenarian life. It's a time of wisdom, experience, and let's face it, a lot of napping. But just because your loved one is in their golden years doesn't mean they can't have fun and be entertained. In fact, with a few simple tweaks, you can make your home a fun and entertaining place for your octogenarian loved one.

First things first, let's talk about games. You know what they say, games are the ultimate cure for boredom. So, let's stock up on some classic board games like Scrabble, Monopoly, and chess. And if your octogenarian loved one is feeling a little more adventurous, you can even introduce them to some newer games like Settlers of Catan or Cards Against Humanity. Just be prepared for some risqué answers from your wise elder.

Next up, let's talk about music. You don't want your octogenarian loved one listening to nothing but Lawrence Welk all day, do you? Of course not! So, let's make sure there's plenty of variety in the music selection. You can create a playlist of their favorite songs, introduce them to some new artists, or even set up a karaoke machine for some sing-alongs. Just make sure you have some earplugs handy for the neighbors.

Now, let's talk about movies and TV shows. You don't want your octogenarian loved one stuck watching nothing but the Weather Channel all day, do you? Of course not! So, let's make sure there's a wide selection of movies and TV shows to choose from. You can invest in a streaming service like Netflix or Hulu, or even introduce them to some classic movies they may have missed like Casablanca or Gone with the Wind.

And finally, let's talk about hobbies. Just because your loved one is in their golden years doesn't mean they can't pick up a new hobby or two. You can introduce them to knitting, painting, or even woodworking. Who knows, maybe they'll become the next Bob Ross or Ron Swanson.

Making your home a fun and entertaining place for your octogenarian loved one is easy and enjoyable. By following these simple steps, you'll be able to create a home that's full of laughter, joy, and maybe even a few inappropriate Cards Against Humanity answers from your wise elder.

Here are a few more ideas for making your home a fun and entertaining place for your octogenarian loved one:

Outdoor Activities: Fresh air and exercise are important at any age, but especially for older adults. Consider setting up a garden or investing in some patio furniture for outdoor relaxation. You can also take them on walks around the neighborhood or local park, or even go on a nature hike if they're up for it.

Cooking and Baking: Cooking and baking can be a fun and creative way to pass the time. You can bake some cookies or cupcakes together, or even try out a new recipe for dinner. And who knows, maybe your loved one will have some secret family recipes to share with you.

Book Clubs: Reading is a great way to stay mentally active and engaged. Consider starting a book club with your loved one and a few other family members or friends. You can read and discuss books together, or even start a mini library in your home.

Movie Nights: Who doesn't love a good movie night? Set up a cozy viewing area in your home with blankets and pillows, and take turns choosing the movies. You can even make some popcorn or other movie snacks to complete the experience.

Intergenerational Activities: Spending time with younger family members can be a great way to keep your loved one feeling young and engaged.

Consider hosting a family game night or taking your loved one to a grandchild's school event. The possibilities are endless!

So there you have it, some ideas for making your home a fun and entertaining place for your octogenarian loved one. Remember, it's important to keep them engaged and stimulated, but also to respect their needs and limitations.

With a little creativity and effort, you can create a home that's enjoyable for everyone.

THE ART OF CAREGIVING

Ah, caregiving for the octogenarian. It's a delicate dance of compassion, patience, and let's be real, a whole lot of poop. But don't worry, my friends. In the art of caregiving for the octogenarian, I'm here to share with you some tips and tricks to make the experience both funny and insightful.

First things first, let's talk about communication. When it comes to caregiving, communication is key. You need to be able to communicate effectively with your loved one, their medical team, and any other caregivers involved. But let's face it, octogenarians can be hard of hearing and may have selective memory. So, make sure to speak clearly, use simple language, and repeat yourself often. And if all else fails, use hand gestures or charades. Just be prepared to get a little silly.

Next up, let's talk about hygiene. Ah, yes, the joys of helping an octogenarian with their personal hygiene. It's not glamorous, but it's a necessary part of caregiving. So, make sure to stock up on plenty of adult diapers, wipes, and other personal care items. And don't forget the importance of hand sanitizer and a strong stomach.

Now, let's talk about nutrition. A healthy diet is important at any age, but especially for the octogenarian. Make sure to provide them with plenty of fruits, vegetables, and lean proteins. But let's be real, sometimes they just want a good old-fashioned piece of cake. And you know what? That's okay. Life is short, and sometimes a little bit of sugar is just what the doctor ordered.

And finally, let's talk about self-care. Caregiving can be exhausting both physically and emotionally. It's important to take care of yourself so that you can be the best caregiver possible. Make sure to take breaks, get plenty of rest, and don't forget to laugh. Laughter really is the best medicine, even if it's at the expense of a well-timed fart from your octogenarian loved one.

So there you have it, my friends. The art of caregiving for the octogenarian is both a challenging and rewarding experience. By following these tips and tricks, you'll be able to provide your loved one with the care they need, while also finding moments of humor and joy in the process.

And who knows, maybe you'll even learn a thing or two about life and love along the way.

Strategies for Providing Physical and Emotional Support

Ah, physical and emotional support for the octogenarian. It's a delicate balance of gentle hugs and not breaking any hips. Let me share with you some strategies for providing physical and emotional support that are both funny and insightful.

Let's start with physical support. One of the biggest challenges of caring for an octogenarian is helping them maintain their independence while also keeping them safe. Here are some tips to help with that balance:

Install grab bars in the bathroom and shower to prevent falls. Just make sure to explain to your octogenarian that they're for holding on to, not pole dancing.

Consider investing in a mobility aid like a walker or cane. But don't be surprised if they name it and start treating it like a member of the family.

Make sure your home is well-lit and free of tripping hazards. But if they do take a spill, make sure to offer plenty of hugs and a humorous anecdote to distract them from any embarrassment.

24

Now let's talk about emotional support. As we age, emotional support becomes just as important as physical support. Here are some strategies for providing emotional support to your octogenarian loved one:

Listen to them. Sometimes all they need is a sympathetic ear to listen to their stories and concerns. But be warned, their stories may involve walking uphill to school both ways, in the snow, with no shoes.

Engage in activities that they enjoy. Whether it's playing a game of cards or watching their favorite TV show, spending time doing something they love can lift their spirits and provide a sense of normalcy.

Make sure they feel loved and appreciated. A simple hug, compliment, or expression of gratitude can go a long way in making your loved one feel valued and cared for.

So there you have it, some strategies for providing physical and emotional support to your octogenarian loved one. Just remember, caregiving can be challenging, but it can also be a rewarding and fulfilling experience. So, embrace the humor, enjoy the moments, and don't forget to give lots of hugs (but be careful not to break any hips).

Here are some additional strategies for providing physical and emotional support to your octogenarian loved one:

Physical Support:

Help them stay active. Exercise is important for maintaining physical health and preventing falls. Encourage your loved one to engage in low-impact activities like walking, swimming, or yoga.

Make sure they're comfortable. As we age, our bodies can become more sensitive to temperature changes. Make sure your loved one is dressed appropriately for the weather and has access to warm blankets and cozy socks.

Assist with daily tasks. Sometimes the little things can be the most challenging for an octogenarian. Offer to help with tasks like grocery shopping, cooking, or cleaning. Just be prepared for them to insist that they can still do it themselves.

Emotional Support:

Encourage socialization. Loneliness can be a major issue for older adults, especially if they're no longer able to drive or get out of the house as much. Encourage your loved one to stay connected with friends and family, and consider arranging regular visits or outings with them.

Help them find purpose. Retirement can be a difficult transition for some older adults who may feel like they've lost their sense of purpose. Encourage your loved one to pursue hobbies, volunteer, or find other ways to stay engaged in the world.

Be patient and understanding. Aging can be a frustrating and difficult process. Be patient and understanding with your loved one, and try to see things from their perspective. A little empathy can go a long way in providing emotional support.

Remember, caring for an octogenarian can be a challenging but rewarding experience. By providing physical and emotional support, you can help your loved one maintain their independence, feel valued and cared for, and continue to enjoy a high quality of life. And who knows, you may even learn a thing or two about resilience, grace, and the importance of a good sense of humor along the way.

Self-Care for Caregivers:
Why it's important and How To Do It

I can tell you that taking care of an octogenarian can be both rewarding and exhausting. That's why it's important for caregivers to practice self-care. And don't worry, I'm not just going to tell you to take a bubble bath (although that's always a good idea). Here are some funny and insightful tips for practicing self-care as a caregiver:

Take a break. This may seem obvious, but it's easier said than done. It's important to take breaks throughout the day, even if it's just a few minutes to sit down and have a cup of tea. And don't feel guilty about it! As a caregiver, you deserve a break.

Get enough sleep. Again, this may seem obvious, but it's easier said than done. Make sure you're getting enough sleep each night, and don't be afraid to take a nap during the day if you need it. Just make sure your octogenarian loved one isn't waiting on you for something important.

Exercise. Exercise is a great way to reduce stress and improve your mood. And it doesn't have to be a full-on gym session. Even a short walk around the block can do wonders for your physical and mental health.

Connect with others. Caregiving can be isolating, so it's important to connect with others. Reach out to friends and family, join a caregiver support group, or even just have a chat with a neighbor. And don't forget to laugh - humor is a great way to reduce stress and boost your mood.

Treat yourself. As a caregiver, you're always putting others first. But it's important to treat yourself every once in a while.

Whether it's buying yourself a little something or indulging in your favorite treat, don't forget to take care of yourself too.

Remember, self-care isn't selfish - it's essential. By taking care of yourself, you'll be better equipped to take care of your octogenarian loved one. And who knows, you may even find that practicing self-care helps you appreciate the little moments of joy and humor that come with caring for an octogenarian. So go ahead, take that bubble bath - you deserve it!

HOW TO KEEP YOUR OCTOGENARIAN ACTIVE AND ENGAGED

I know that keeping your octogenarian loved one active and engaged is crucial for their physical and mental wellbeing. But how do you do it? Here are some funny and insightful tips for keeping your octogenarian active and engaged:

Get them moving. Exercise is important for maintaining physical health and preventing falls. Encourage your loved one to engage in low-impact activities like walking, swimming, or yoga. But remember, they're not training for the Olympics - it's okay if they're not breaking a sweat.

Give them a purpose. Many older adults feel like they've lost their sense of purpose. Help your loved one find a sense of purpose by encouraging them to pursue hobbies, volunteer, or find other ways to stay engaged in the world. And don't be afraid to get creative - maybe they've always wanted to learn how to paint, or maybe they'd love to start a book club.

Keep them social. Loneliness can be a major issue for older adults, especially if they're no longer able to drive or get out of the house as much. Encourage your loved one to stay connected with friends and family, and consider arranging regular visits or outings with them. And who knows, maybe you'll even make some new friends along the way.

Challenge their minds. Keeping your loved one mentally engaged is just as important as keeping them physically active. Encourage them to do crossword puzzles, play games, or read books. And don't be afraid to introduce them to new things - maybe they'll love learning how to use a tablet or listening to podcasts.

Make it fun. Let's face it - nobody wants to do something if it's not fun. So find ways to make staying active and engaged fun for your loved one. Maybe you can turn a walk around the neighborhood into a scavenger hunt, or turn a boring chore into a game. Just don't be surprised if your loved one starts beating you at your own game.

Remember, keeping your octogenarian loved one active and engaged isn't just important for their physical and mental health - it's also a great way to spend quality time with them. So get creative, have fun, and enjoy the journey together!

Here are some additional tips for keeping your octogenarian loved one active and engaged:

Encourage them to learn something new. Learning a new skill or hobby can be a great way to stay engaged and mentally sharp. Encourage your loved one to try something they've always been interested in but never had the chance to pursue, such as learning a new language or taking a cooking class.

Embrace technology. Technology can be intimidating for older adults, but it can also be a great way to stay connected with family and friends, access information, and stay engaged in the world. Help your loved one get comfortable with technology by setting up video calls, showing them how to use social media, or finding other ways to incorporate technology into their daily routine.

Incorporate mindfulness practices. Mindfulness practices, such as meditation or yoga, can be a great way to reduce stress and anxiety and promote overall wellbeing.

Encourage your loved one to try these practices and incorporate them into their daily routine.

Get them involved in community activities. Many communities offer programs and activities specifically for older adults, such as senior centers or exercise classes. Encourage your loved one to get involved in these activities and meet new people.

Be patient and supportive. Remember that every person is different, and what works for one person may not work for another. Be patient and supportive as your loved one explores different activities and finds what works best for them. And most importantly, remember to have fun and enjoy the time you spend together!

Creative ideas for Activities and Hobbies

Finding creative activities and hobbies for your octogenarian loved one can be a challenge. But fear not - with a little imagination and a good sense of humor, you can come up with some fun and engaging ideas. Here are some funny and insightful suggestions for activities and hobbies that your octogenarian loved one might enjoy:

Become a detective. Encourage your loved one to put their sleuthing skills to the test by reading mystery novels or watching detective shows. Who knows, maybe they'll even solve a real-life mystery in their neighborhood!

Get crafty. Crafts are a great way to stay engaged and creative. Encourage your loved one to take up knitting, crocheting, or scrapbooking. Not only will they create something beautiful, but they'll also have a sense of accomplishment when they finish their project.

Embrace their inner child. Just because your loved one is older doesn't mean they can't have fun like a kid. Encourage them to play board games, build a puzzle, or even have a tea party with friends.

Try something new. There's no age limit on trying something new. Encourage your loved one to explore new hobbies or activities, like learning a new language, taking a dance class, or even trying their hand at painting.

Get outdoors. Fresh air and sunshine can do wonders for a person's mood and wellbeing. Encourage your loved one to spend time outside by gardening, bird watching, or even just going for a walk around the neighborhood.

Explore technology. Technology can be intimidating for older adults, but it can also be a great way to stay connected and engaged in the world. Encourage your loved one to explore technology by learning how to use a tablet, joining a virtual book club, or even playing games on their phone.

Take a trip down memory lane. Encourage your loved one to share their life stories and memories with you. You could even help them create a scrapbook or photo album to document their life and experiences.

Remember, the key to finding creative activities and hobbies for your octogenarian loved one is to keep an open mind and have fun. And who knows, maybe you'll even discover a new hobby or activity that you enjoy together!

Here are some more creative ideas for activities and hobbies that your octogenarian loved one might enjoy:

Volunteer. Encourage your loved one to give back to the community by volunteering. They could volunteer at a local animal shelter, hospital, or soup kitchen, or even participate in a charity walk or fundraiser.

Join a book club. Reading is a great way to stay engaged and learn new things. Encourage your loved one to join a book club or start one of their own. They can meet new people and have fun discussing their favorite books.

Cook and bake. Cooking and baking are great ways to stay active and engaged. Encourage your loved one to try new recipes or even teach you some of their favorite family recipes. You could even have a cook-off to see who can make the best dish!

Attend cultural events. Many cities and towns offer cultural events like concerts, plays, and art exhibits. Encourage your loved one to attend these events and experience something new.

Play games. Games are a fun and engaging way to spend time together. Encourage your loved one to play cards, dominoes, or even video games. You could even host a game night with friends and family.

Learn about history. History is full of fascinating stories and events. Encourage your loved one to explore history by reading historical books or watching documentaries. They could even visit historical sites or museums.

Stay active. Exercise is important for physical and mental wellbeing. Encourage your loved one to stay active by taking walks, practicing yoga, or even dancing. You could even join a fitness class together.

Remember, the most important thing is to find activities and hobbies that your loved one enjoys and that help them stay engaged and fulfilled. With a little creativity and a sense of humor, you can find the perfect activity for your octogenarian loved one.

Staying Connected with Friends and Family

Ah, staying connected with friends and family is an important aspect of keeping your octogenarian loved one happy and fulfilled. Here are some funny yet insightful tips on how to do it:

Phone a friend. Encourage your loved one to pick up the phone and call their friends and family members. Hearing a friendly voice can brighten their day and keep them connected.

Use technology. Technology can be intimidating for some seniors, but it can also be a great way to stay connected. Teach your loved one how to use video chat platforms like Zoom or Skype to have virtual visits with friends and family.

Send snail mail. In today's world of instant gratification, receiving a handwritten letter or card in the mail can be a delightful surprise. Encourage your loved one to send letters to friends and family or even join a pen pal program.

Host a gathering. Whether it's a small dinner party or a big family reunion, hosting a gathering is a great way to bring friends and family together. Encourage your loved one to host their own gathering or help them plan one.

Attend community events. Many communities offer events like festivals, concerts, and holiday celebrations. Encourage your loved one to attend these events and connect with others in their community.

Join a club or group. Whether it's a book club, a gardening group, or a knitting circle, joining a club or group is a great way to meet new people and stay connected. Encourage your loved one to find a group that interests them and join in on the fun.

Remember, staying connected with friends and family is important for emotional wellbeing and happiness. With a little creativity and effort, you can help your octogenarian loved one stay connected and engaged with the people they love.

Here are some more funny yet insightful tips on how to help your octogenarian loved one stay connected with friends and family:

Share photos and memories. Encourage your loved one to share old photos and memories with friends and family. This can spark conversations and help them feel connected to their loved ones.

Plan a trip. Whether it's a short weekend getaway or a longer vacation, planning a trip with friends or family can be a great way to stay connected. Encourage your loved one to plan a trip with their loved ones and make some new memories together.

Attend church or religious services. For those who are religious, attending church or religious services can be a great way to stay connected with their community. Encourage your loved one to attend services regularly and participate in church activities.

Use social media. Social media platforms like Facebook and Twitter can be a great way to stay connected with friends and family, especially those who live far away. Encourage your loved one to create a social media account and connect with their loved ones online.

Play games together. Playing games together is a great way to bond with friends and family. Encourage your loved one to play games like Scrabble, chess, or even video games with their loved ones.

Host a potluck. A potluck is a fun and easy way to bring friends and family together. Encourage your loved one to host a potluck and have everyone bring their favorite dish to share.

Remember, staying connected with friends and family is important for overall wellbeing and happiness. By encouraging your octogenarian loved one to stay in touch with their loved ones, you can help them feel more fulfilled and engaged with the world around them.

HUMOROUS TALES AND REFLECTIONS ON CAREGIVING

Caregiving for an octogenarian can certainly provide some humorous moments and reflections. Here are some funny yet insightful tales and reflections from an expert caregiver:

The power of persuasion. I once spent hours trying to convince my octogenarian loved one to take a shower. After many unsuccessful attempts, I finally resorted to telling her that George Clooney was coming over for dinner and she needed to be presentable. Miraculously, she was in the shower within minutes.

The great escape. My octogenarian loved one once decided to take matters into her own hands and escape from her assisted living facility. She was found strolling down the street in her bathrobe, carrying a bag of candy she had swiped from the nurses' station. Needless to say, we had a good laugh about it once she was safely back in her room.

The magic of music. I discovered that music can be a powerful tool for engaging with my octogenarian loved one. One day, we were listening to some oldies on the radio and she started singing along to "Can't Buy Me Love" by The Beatles. It was a joy to see her come alive and connect with the music in such a positive way.

The joys of companionship. Spending time with my octogenarian loved one has taught me the importance of companionship. Even if we're just sitting together, reading a book or watching TV, the simple act of being there with her brings us both joy and comfort.

The little things matter. I've learned that the little things can make a big difference in the life of an octogenarian. Something as simple as a warm blanket or a favorite treat can brighten their day and make them feel loved and cared for.

Funny Stories and Anecdotes About Life With an Octogenarian

Here are some funny stories and anecdotes about life with an octogenarian:

The disappearing remote control. My octogenarian loved one had a habit of misplacing the TV remote control. One day, we found it in the fridge, and we still have no idea how it got there!

The endless naptime. My loved one would often fall asleep while watching TV, and it was a challenge to wake her up. We tried everything from gentle nudges to loud noises, but she would always manage to drift back off.

The unexpected phone call. My octogenarian loved one had a habit of calling me at the most unexpected times, like when I was in the middle of a meeting or taking a shower. It was always a surprise, but I couldn't help but laugh at her timing.

The stubborn streak. My loved one had a stubborn streak, and it often resulted in humorous disagreements.

One time, she refused to wear her glasses, insisting that she could see just fine without them. Needless to say, she ended up knocking over a vase!

The unexpected guest. One day, a squirrel made its way into the house through an open window. My loved one was delighted by the unexpected visitor and spent the next half-hour feeding it nuts.

The misplaced hearing aid. My loved one had a habit of misplacing her hearing aid, and we often found it in the most unexpected places, like in the couch cushions or under her pillow. One time, we even found it in the dog's bed!

The forgetful moment. My loved one had a moment of forgetfulness and accidentally put her shoes in the fridge instead of the pantry. We still laugh about it to this day.

The quirky habits. My octogenarian loved one had some quirky habits, like singing along to every song on the radio or insisting on using a certain brand of dish soap. It was these little quirks that made her so endearing.

The unexpected talent. My loved one surprised us all when she revealed that she had a talent for knitting. She spent the next few weeks knitting scarves and hats for everyone in the family.

The competitive streak. My octogenarian loved one had a competitive streak, and it often came out during game nights. She would become fiercely competitive, even during friendly games of Scrabble or Monopoly.

The fashion statement. My loved one had a unique sense of style and would often mix and match patterns and colors in unexpected ways. One time, she wore a polka dot shirt with striped pants, and we couldn't help but laugh.

The adventurous spirit. My octogenarian loved one had an adventurous spirit, and she always wanted to try new things. One time, she convinced us to go bungee jumping with her!

The baking mishap. My loved one loved to bake, but one time, she accidentally put salt instead of sugar in a cake recipe. Needless to say, it didn't turn out quite as expected.

The prankster. My octogenarian loved one had a mischievous side and would often play pranks on us.

One time, she convinced us that the house was haunted by moving furniture around while we were out.

The dancing queen. My loved one loved to dance, and she was always the life of the party.

One time, she got up on the table and started dancing to "Jailhouse Rock" at a family gathering.

The unexpected talent (part 2). My octogenarian loved one surprised us again when she revealed that she was an expert at origami. She spent hours creating intricate paper designs, and we were all impressed by her skill.

The adventurous eater. My loved one was always willing to try new foods, no matter how unusual or exotic they might be. One time, she even tried deep-fried insects while on a trip to Thailand!

The forgetful moment (part 2). My octogenarian loved one had another forgetful moment when she accidentally put dish soap in the dishwasher instead of detergent. The resulting bubble explosion was quite the sight!

The tech-savvy octogenarian. My loved one surprised us all when she became an expert at using social media.

She would post daily updates and pictures of her adventures, and we all enjoyed following along.

The sweet tooth. My octogenarian loved one had a serious sweet tooth and would often sneak candy and cookies when she thought no one was looking. It was hard to resist her puppy-dog eyes when caught in the act.

In summary, life with an octogenarian can be filled with funny and unexpected moments. It's these moments that make caregiving such a rewarding and fulfilling experience.

Insights and Wisdom Gained From Caring For an Elderly Loved One

I've gained a lot of insights and wisdom that I never would have expected. Here are some of my favorite observations:

Life is precious. When you spend time caring for an octogenarian, you quickly realize how precious life is.

It's a reminder to appreciate every moment and not take anything for granted.

Patience is key. Caring for an elderly loved one can be challenging, but it requires a lot of patience. You learn to take a step back and see things from their perspective, which can be incredibly enlightening.

Laughter is the best medicine. When things get tough, a little laughter can go a long way. Sharing a joke or a funny story with your loved one can help lift their spirits and make the day a little brighter.

Memories are priceless. Spending time with an octogenarian is a great opportunity to learn about their life experiences and the memories they've made along the way. You gain a newfound appreciation for the richness and diversity of life.

Compassion and empathy are important. Caring for an octogenarian requires a lot of compassion and empathy. You learn to put yourself in their shoes and understand their needs, which helps strengthen your bond and deepen your relationship.

Family is everything. When caring for an octogenarian, you realize the importance of family. You come together to support each other and make sure your loved one is taken care of. It's a reminder of the power of love and connection.

It's okay to ask for help. Caregiving can be overwhelming, and it's important to remember that it's okay to ask for help. Whether it's from family, friends, or professional caregivers, reaching out for support can make a world of difference.

Aging is a privilege. Caring for an octogenarian is a reminder that aging is a privilege. It's an opportunity to live a long and fulfilling life and to share that life with the people you love.

Every person is unique. One of the most important things I've learned is that every octogenarian is unique. Each person has their own personality, interests, and needs, and it's important to get to know them as individuals. By doing so, you can provide personalized care that meets their specific needs and preferences.

Small moments matter. When caring for an octogenarian, it's the small moments that often matter the most.

A simple hug, a kind word, or a shared memory can make all the difference in the world. These small moments can help you connect with your loved one on a deeper level and create cherished memories that will last a lifetime.

Mindfulness is key. Caregiving can be stressful, and it's important to practice mindfulness to stay present in the moment and reduce stress.

Taking a deep breath, practicing meditation or yoga, or simply taking a walk can help you stay centered and focused.

Flexibility is important. When caring for an octogenarian, things don't always go according to plan.

It's important to be flexible and adaptable, and to be willing to adjust your plans as needed. This can help reduce stress and make caregiving more manageable.

Communication is essential. Effective communication is essential when caring for an octogenarian. It's important to listen actively, speak clearly and respectfully, and be open to feedback. By doing so, you can build trust, strengthen your relationship, and provide better care.

It's never too late to learn something new. Caring for an octogenarian can be an opportunity to learn new skills and gain new insights. Whether it's learning a new hobby or listening to stories about the past, there's always something new to discover.

Gratitude is key. Finally, caring for an octogenarian teaches you the importance of gratitude. By focusing on the positive and expressing gratitude for the moments you share together, you can cultivate a sense of joy and appreciation that can help sustain you through the ups and downs of caregiving.

Caring for an octogenarian is a transformative experience that teaches you about the beauty and fragility of life. It's an opportunity to gain wisdom, compassion, and empathy, and to appreciate the moments that make life worth living.

CONCLUSION

As we reach the end of this book, it's important to remember that caring for an octogenarian is both a privilege and a challenge. While it can be rewarding to spend time with our loved ones and provide them with the care they need, it can also be stressful, overwhelming, and emotionally draining.

But by approaching caregiving with a sense of humor, compassion, and creativity, we can create a safe and supportive environment that promotes physical and emotional well-being. From adapting our homes to the needs of our loved ones to staying connected with friends and family, there are countless strategies we can use to provide the best possible care for our octogenarians.

So, let's embrace the journey of caregiving with open hearts and open minds. Let's appreciate the moments of joy, the unexpected lessons, and the humor that can arise in even the most challenging of situations. And let's remember that while caring for an octogenarian can be a difficult task, it is also an opportunity to show our love and appreciation for the people who have shaped our lives and made us who we are today.

Why Octogenarians Need Special Care

Ah, octogenarians - those wise and wonderful creatures who have lived through decades of life, love, and laughter. While they are undoubtedly full of wisdom and experience, they also have unique needs when it comes to care.

First of all, let's talk about the obvious - the physical changes that come with aging. As we get older, our bodies start to slow down, and we become more prone to things like falls, fractures, and chronic health conditions. Octogenarians may also struggle with vision and hearing loss, mobility issues, and cognitive changes like dementia.

But it's not just physical health that needs special attention - emotional well-being is also crucial. Octogenarians may face social isolation and loneliness as they lose friends and loved ones, and they may also struggle with feelings of anxiety, depression, or grief.

So, what can we do to provide the special care that octogenarians need? First of all, we need to approach caregiving with patience, empathy, and a sense of humor. We need to adapt our homes and daily routines to meet their unique needs, while also encouraging them to stay active, engaged, and connected to the world around them.

Above all, we need to remember that octogenarians are people, with their own quirks, preferences, and personalities. By listening to their stories, sharing our own experiences, and creating a safe and supportive environment, we can give them the care and attention they deserve in their golden years.

So, here's to our octogenarian loved ones - may they continue to live their lives to the fullest, with all the care, love, and laughter they need along the way.

The Importance of Humor and Compassion in Caregiving

Ah, humor and compassion - two essential ingredients in the recipe for great caregiving. When it comes to caring for our loved ones, whether they're octogenarians or not, it's important to remember that laughter and empathy can be just as powerful as medicine or therapy.

First of all, let's talk about humor. As they say, laughter is the best medicine - and this is especially true for seniors.

A good joke or silly story can lighten the mood, reduce stress, and improve overall well-being. Plus, sharing a laugh can help to build stronger bonds between caregivers and care recipients, creating a sense of closeness and trust.

Of course, humor needs to be used sensitively and appropriately - there's a time and a place for a good joke, and it's important to be mindful of your loved one's emotional state and sense of humor. But with a little bit of care and attention, you can find ways to bring joy and laughter into their lives.

Now, let's talk about compassion. Caregiving can be a challenging and emotional experience, and it's easy to get caught up in the stress and pressure of it all. But it's important to remember that your loved one is a person, with their own thoughts, feelings, and struggles.

By showing compassion - that is, by putting yourself in their shoes, listening to their concerns, and responding with kindness and understanding - you can create a sense of safety and comfort that can be just as important as physical care.

Whether it's holding their hand during a difficult moment or simply offering a listening ear, small gestures of compassion can make a big difference in their lives.

So, whether you're caring for an octogenarian or anyone else, remember the power of humor and compassion. By bringing joy and empathy into your caregiving, you can create a more meaningful, fulfilling, and joyful experience for everyone involved.

Made in the USA
Columbia, SC
10 March 2023